The Wizard of OZ Counting

by Kristen McCurry

illustrated by Timothy Banks

CAPSTONE PRESS

a capstone imprint

1

ONE little girl
has lost her way.
Can you help Dorothy
count today?

2

2

In the Land of Oz,
TWO witches alight.
One is kind.
The other is a fright!

3

THREE friends she meets
on the road again—
a scarecrow, a lion,
and a man made of tin.

On **FOUR** little legs,
Toto runs very fast
from the Wicked Witch
and the spells that she casts.

8

5

Look out! Winged monkeys!
Run for your lives!
How many do you see?
Dorothy counts FIVE.

6

SIX friendly Munchkins,
all miniature sizes—

the Land of Oz
is full of surprises!

7

SEVEN Winkie guards—
the Wicked Witch they must obey.

Dorothy sets them free.
The Winkies say, "Hooray!"

8

Scarecrow, Cowardly Lion,
Dorothy, and Tin Man

skip with **EIGHT** feet
as fast as they can.

9

NINE wild poppies
make Dorothy want to snooze.
Hurry to the Wizard!
There's no time to lose!

10

TEN towers in Emerald City—
the friends' journey is through!
Courage, brain, heart, and home—
wishes do come true!

About the Wizard of Oz

The Wizard of Oz follows young Dorothy Gale and her little dog, Toto, who are magically taken by tornado from Kansas to the Land of Oz. Dorothy sets off on the yellow brick road and meets the Scarecrow, Tin Man, and Cowardly Lion. They join her on a dangerous journey to meet the Wizard of Oz, whose powers may help Dorothy return home.

The Wizard of Oz is one of the most beloved stories of all time. The book was written by L. Frank Baum and published in 1900. The tale has been told and retold countless times in books and in movies.

Glossary

alight—to land on something

cast—to put forth or throw

emerald—a bright green precious stone

miniature—much smaller than usual size

poppy—a flowering plant

spell—words believed to have magical powers

wicked—very evil or mean

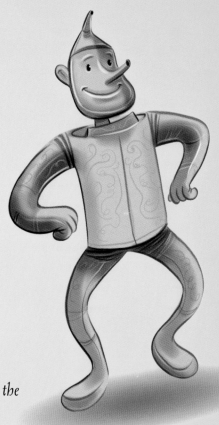

Read More

Lee, Mark, and Kurt Cyrus. *Twenty Big Trucks in the Middle of the Street.* Somerville, Mass.: Candlewick Press, 2013.

MacDonald, Margaret Read. *How Many Donkeys? An Arabic Counting Tale.* New York: AV2 by Weigl, 2012.

Rissman, Rebecca. *Counting in the Ocean.* I Can Count! Chicago: Heinemann Library, 2013.

Internet Sites

FactHound offers a safe, fun way to find Internet sites related to this book. All of the sites on FactHound have been researched by our staff.

Here's all you do:

Visit *www.facthound.com*

Type in this code: 9781476537665

Super-cool stuff! Check out projects, games and lots more at www.capstonekids.com

Published in 2014 by Capstone Press
1710 Roe Crest Drive
North Mankato, Minnesota 56003
www.capstonepub.com

Library of Congress Cataloging-in-Publication Data
McCurry, Kristen.
The Wizard of Oz counting / by Kristen McCurry;
illustrated by Timothy Banks.
pages cm — (The Wizard of Oz)
Summary: "Simple rhyming text and full-color illustrations introduce counting 1 to 10 using The Wizard of Oz"— Provided by publisher.
Audience: 6–7. Audience: K to grade 3.
Includes bibliographical references and index.
ISBN 978-1-4765-3766-5 (library binding)
ISBN 978-1-4765-3770-2 (board book)
ISBN 978-1-4765-3778-8 (ebook pdf)
1. Counting—Juvenile literature. 2. Arithmetic—Juvenile literature. I. Banks, Timothy, illustrator. II. Title. III. Title: Counting.
QA113.M3934 2014
513.2'1—dc23   2013009527

Editorial Credits
Gillia Olson, editor; Ted Williams, designer; Nathan Gassman, art director; Eric Manske, production specialist

Index

Look for all the books in the series:

Printed in the United States of America in North Mankato, Minnesota.
032013   007223CGF13

E MCCUR   FLT
McCurry, Kristen,
The Wizard of Oz counting /

01/15